AF152418

YOUR KNOWLEDGE HAS VALUE

- We will publish your bachelor's and master's thesis, essays and papers

- Your own eBook and book - sold worldwide in all relevant shops

- Earn money with each sale

Upload your text at www.GRIN.com
and publish for free

Bibliographic information published by the German National Library:

The German National Library lists this publication in the National Bibliography; detailed bibliographic data are available on the Internet at http://dnb.dnb.de .

Imprint:

Copyright © 2016 GRIN Verlag, Open Publishing GmbH
Print and binding: Books on Demand GmbH, Norderstedt Germany
ISBN: 9783656987024

This book at GRIN:

http://www.grin.com/en/e-book/336987/christianity-islam-and-judaism-a-review-of-the-abrahamic-faiths

Emmanuel Wayi

Christianity, Islam and Judaism. A Review of the Abrahamic Faiths

As Presented By Philip Sheldrake

GRIN Publishing

CHRISTIANITY, ISLAM AND JUDAISM. A REVIEW OF THE ABRAHAMIC FAITHS AS PRESENTED BY PHILIP SHELDRAKE

INTRODUCTION

Philip Sheldrake presents his work on the spiritualities of the three biggest world's faith in some sort of a defined outline. In all three chapters, there may be some position change in the way the topics appear but the framework is the same. He seeks to show the origin of a particular spirituality, the teachings, the sources and how the life in each is led. In all, he tries to show some aspects of the ascetic life and mysticism and whether each has got a particular attention to world mission. The conclusion is often the summary of the whole chapter in a nutshell.

JEWISH SPIRITUALITY

The author begins by presenting Judaism as a religion intended for faith and ethnic identity. This faith can be grouped into two denominations or forms namely: The Sephardic (in the Middle East) and the Ashkenazi found all over Europe. These different groups seek to re-read the Jewish traditions in contemporary understanding. He presents Judaism as the parent of the "Abrahamic Faith" since the other two main religions, Islam and Christianity recognize Abraham as their prototype. This faith can be traced as far back as 3000-4000 years around the Mesopotamia area. The Jews trace their history alongside that of their faith in which God interacted with them as the chosen people.

In this chapter, Sheldrake presents the Jewish spirituality as being active-practical, meaning that it is a daily affair. It is practical, ethical and daily-present and it hardly builds on certain doctrines but rather flowing from the observance of the law. It is more of a communal than an individual affair even though the individual has the right to a personal response to God who guided and protected them from the past to a holy live today. It is the stand on the fact that God relates to human affairs which is contrary to the atheist idea that God is detached from the world. Judaism holds on to monotheism and hopes for the messiah who shall come to restore Israel to its glory.

The source of this spirituality is the Torah, the Talmud and even the Midrash, but there had also been some outside influences. They view life as better if it is lived by getting involved with others outside Judaism. They may view ascetic life as a source of regeneration but they do not hold to monasticism. Daily prayers and weekly Sabbath retreats prepare them for mission to the world considered as the "tikkum olam". The reading of the scripture is paramount and the Temple is the holy place for worship. There are also Jewish sects and they believe in mysticism. For the Jews, God cannot be known fully but there are forces such as, wisdom, kindness, love etc. by which God connects to the world and these forces must not be regarded as gods. All worship belong to one God the creator.

BIAS

In the author's presentation of Judaism there seem to be the desire to emphasize positions as to who is first or last or who is parent and who is a child between the three faiths. Seeing Judaism as the parent faith to the two others is slightly an error that may spark up another sentimental discussion between the faiths. If Abraham is the source of all the faiths then none can claim to have been the mother of the other. I personally resent the idea of placing any one faith as the mother or father of the others. Abraham is their one source and it is better left that way.

WHAT'S NEW

From the work of this author, I have been able to learn of the fact that Judaism also has denominations and also the fact that they believe in a mission to the world through the "tikkum olam". I must also say that it was quite informative to here that there are more Jews outside than they are in Israel. It intrigued me to know that the Jews believe in the "Redeemer" and "Messiah". I now know that their belief in the Messiah is of one who will come to restore the "glory of Israel" surely as a chosen people, politically. It is also good to know that the Jews are receptive to outsiders since they see it as a divine duty.

MUSLIM SPIRITUALITY

The author presents the Muslim spirituality as a daily affair often done in houses by families. It is grounded on the dictates of the Qur'an and the textual sayings of Muhammad. The Kaaba is their center of worship. Life as a whole is spiritual and not just a simple act or practice of spirituality. There is no different between a spiritual and a secular life. They hold on to monotheism and on the five pillars of Islam as the basic rituals of spirituality. There are also two major denominations of Islam; the Sunni and the Shia which are not separated by belief but by lineage. Islam embraces the outside faiths through the community known as the "ummah". The teachings of Islam are creedal and are seen as a culmination of the revelation from Abraham, Moses, and Jesus to Muhammad, the last of the prophets.

There is not the belief in priest or pastor to serve as mediators between the people and God. The individual has a certain privilege connection with Allah. Charity and compassion are the components of the journey to heaven. Monasticism is ignored but daily prayers are encouraged.

A BAIS AND WHAT IS LACKING OF CHRISTIANITY

It is not fair for me that the author says Islam seem to view itself as the fulfilment of all past revelation. This means that they see themselves as the correction of all past errors and the fulfilment of all past correctness. It is a claim of superiority which I think is not necessary in matters of faith. Secondly, the author says "Islam is fiercely monotheistic". Even though the usage of the word 'fiercely' may refer to the strong belief in one God, it may be misinterpreted to mean violence. I think the usage of the word is wrong. Thirdly the author present Islam as opposed to the Christian doctrine of the Trinity as polytheistic. I think his work wanted to show more of the similarities than the differences in the spiritualities of the three religions. It is certainly not true that the Trinity is polytheistic in the Christian sense.

WHAT'S NEW

From this work I have learned a new word in Islam. I was told back home that the theologians of Islam were referred to as the "Modibo" but by this I have learnt of the "Ayatollahs" of the Shia Muslims. Again I have learnt that Christianity and Islam are closed to each other in matters of saintship (intercession), the belief in angels, the resurrection, original sin and even miracles. And lastly, that the two forms of Islam are not divided by belief but by lineage.

CHRISTIAN SPIRITUALITY

According to the author, Christianity has four main denominations or forms which came about as a result of schism in theology and institutions. It is born out of Jewish monotheism and the bible is the source of its spirituality especially the New Testament and later doctrines. Also, it takes the concept of discipleship in to account which involves the following of the way of Jesus which is also a radical breaking with one's past. It teaches about the incarnated Christ and the indwelling of the spirit in the heart of man. The Christian life is communal and not individualistic. Membership is by Baptism and the post resurrection experience holds a great part in this spirituality. Monasticism is found and martyrdom seemed to have accompanied the faith for long. This spirituality has sought to adjust to contemporary events and each context develops its own response by their various social and cultural contexts such as liberation, feminist etc. Today, this spirituality has extended to the rise of the ecumenical movements searching for a peaceful dialogue between Christianity and other religions.

BIAS AND LACK OF INFORMATION IN CHRISTIANITY

I do not think that the search for a peaceful dialogue has been an exclusive activity of Christianity. There are other faiths that have been receptive to this idea and if this can be reckon to Christianity as a form of spirituality, then it must also be reckoned to the other faiths that have embraced the idea. Secondly, the author fails to see that there are other recent forms of Christianity such as the Pentecostal and the African Instituted Churches and the Tele-Evangelical Ministries which are completely different from what he simply calls the Churches of the Reformation. Thirdly, the various recent contextual responses to Christian spirituality have not been fully explored as the author limited himself only to the south of America and Europe. There have been different forms of such struggles in Africa and Asia too. The liberation cry in South America over the issue of poverty is not the same as the cry against colonialism, corruption or Apartheid in Africa.

WHAT'S NEW

I have learned to understand that spirituality goes beyond a simple individual prayer to a general commitment to the faiths of the world. I never could understand that the ecumenical movements were into Christian spirituality. I have often seen these words to mean a private devotion time in a private place like a hill or a monastery etc.

CONCLUSION

Philip Sheldrake choses to present the various faiths from the point of their spiritualities. In whatever ways he looked at these, I see that the author tries so hard to avoid doctrinal issues which have always been the points of divide between the various faiths. For me, this author has rather presented some commonness within the different faiths by trying to link them to one origin which is Abraham and to a common phenomenon in the practice of the faiths. He seems to show that there are various common themes that run through all the faiths which are mysticism, asceticism and world mission. It means that to a certain extent all these faith have components of mission even if there are not fully shown. It wasn't possible for me before to know that the "tikkum olam" of the Jews or the "ummah" of the Muslim were almost the same as the ecumenical movements of Christianity. But now there is a different view all together.

REFERENCE

Sheldrake, Philip. *Spirituality: A Guide for the Perplexed. London, GBR: Bloomsbury Academic, 2014. ProQuest ebrary. Web. 14 April 2015.*